An Occasional Gentleman's NOTES

Joe LoCascio

Copyright © 2023 Joe LoCascio
All Rights Reserved

First Edition, First Printing — April 2023
Library of Congress Control Number: 2023930961
ISBN 978-1-953136-49-7   Hardback
ISBN 978-1-953136-48-0   Paperback

Cover Design by **Pierian Springs Press**
Cover Art by Lumezia, licensed from Adobe, Inc
Cover Page *Bauhaus Dessau* **Alfarn** by Céline Hurka,
Elia Preuss, Flavia Zimbardi,
Hidetaka Yamasaki, and Luca Pellegrini.
Flourishes set in Emigre Foundry **Dalliance**, by Frank Heine
Emigre Foundry **ZeitGuys**, by Bob Aufuldish, Eric Donelan
Typefaces licensed Adobe, Linotype, & URW GmbH

PierianSpringsPress.Com
Sheridan, Wyoming

For Lucia

Poems

black pierrot	1
the players	2
recalling jimmy c	3
the three	4
bill evans	5
of healing	6
procol harum	7
the improviser	8
via crucis	9
incidental music	10
structure	11
the standard	12
other angles	14
variations	15
the man in the black suit	16
blackout	17
the fall	18
red	20
the wind	21
eugene	22
hannah	24
post-funeral	25
nothing by it	26
tonight	27
oh, but our own	28
good morning	29
elusive memory	30
portrait in two yellows	31
the florist	32
neutral adhesive	33
bridgeport	34
requiem for a jazz club	46
modern english	50
exercises for independence of the fingers	51
fats waller	52
grandmother	53
father	54

stone idol ... 55
an occasional gentleman ... 56
like gieseking playing scarlatti ... 57
faceless in texas ... 58
a wave of despair ... 59
when i write music ... 60
ecology ... 62
in our greed ... 63
sudden heart ... 64
eulogy ... 65

Lyrics

flamingos ... 69
st. john ... 70
la divina ... 71
eugene ... 72
again ... 74
Lovecraft On The Beach ... 75
For You ... 76
One I Hope to Love ... 78
Ghosts ... 79
Paralyzed ... 80
Not Far Away ... 82
A Widow's Tale ... 83
Sideshow ... 84
Comes the Rain ... 85
Scary People ... 86
Ms. Thing ... 87

Acknowledgments ... 89

About the Author ... 91

Also by Joe LoCascio ... 93

An Occasional Gentleman's NOTES

Poems

black pierrot

the texas twister.
don wilkerson—
there was that night at lott's
jazz cafe when that big time
so and so saxophonist sat
in with the band

and you showed up lookin' like an
undernourished alley cat.
Lookin' beautiful.

no bread, borrowed horn,
just enough left to make it up
to the stage. then horn, lips
and heart converged.
mystery and magic flowed again.

that big time saxophonist's
recording contract couldn't save him
from the carving up he took from
you that night.

you once said
man was not meant
to walk upright—
something do with the
weight of the organs.

the last time I heard you play
I thought to myself: makes the
tenor saxophone cry. makes it wail
like a cello. as long as you have a horn
to play,

I'll be listening,
down on all fours.

the players

    hover like race horses   lean and intent
    conquerers of fear and denial   in the music
                                        through the music
          often eluding their strained hands;
        gall keeps them awake
                  keeps them humble
                at the altar
  where the bones of ellington   mingus parker
armstrong
     beiderbecke   davis gillespie
          navarro   evans   (gil & bill)

        coltrane   basie   hawkins
            young   holiday
          and tristano
        reside and savagely hum.

recalling jimmy c

think long ago
before idealism

turned to trivia:
we blazed away

not wise
nor defeated

only maddened
with youth.

the three

what was best
      was when you would
imitate the old italian lady
      who smelled of mothballs—
nick and i would
      laugh till we hurt.
      you captured the inflections
of her speech, her movements:
      the way she would suck
      at her teeth—too much,
          really too much.
             when
time was running out we asked
      you to do the imitation
once more and you did.
      it was your finest performance,
one even the
      old lady would
have applauded. we were quite
        a team, you,
        nick and me
        that night—
your eyes aglow with pride, willing
to accept the swing of the cancers' scythe,
unwilling to bow to it without great bales
of laughter and mockery to cushion the blow.

bill evans

he put
the ideal of
paul klee
into music

took
the line
for a walk
then
made it dance

of healing

the magic
the jazz
is fading away
as we wave banners
and concoct picnics
incredibly forgetting
our child is alone
and about to step
           off the pier

procol harum

your tales of dissipation/isolation:
      your mad captains—
bloated feasts—
junky doctors—   pearls from the orient
        placed in a world moving
     slippery through the ghostly organ,
           the cynical piano—
coddled in snare drum promiscuity.
            from the early morning fandango
to the midnight sarabande
     there has always been a place
        for one to come and disappear
          into deep gauzes
              beyond barricades
        closing the sea   between
                ourselves
 and the quest for
     a simple grace

the improviser

as my father believed
was not necessarily a

person creating brilliant works
fed from rivers of inspiration

as much as a person simply
making what was readily available

functional

via crucis

accepting passion
vile and wonderful

electric in a haze
sweet and horrible

shooting our love
into green-stemmed hope
we drown in music

incidental music

                    sweat on a fingertip
faith by the windowpane
                    breath to a windmill
light for the hunger
                food for the eye

green green green: you tell yourself
go go go
              light the fire
eat the fire   burn in and out
get out out out   touch the distance
                then plop yourself
on the kitchen floor
                    and talk rabies to the dog

structure
> *for r.c.*

to someone by the door
glaring wildly at me

(or maybe madly at me) i
give a superficial sign.

a breeze resurrects passion
i wished had left long ago—

toys lolling in the wind,
a recalled slight, such old wounds

could hardly be counted
to tame the night. remember me,

think me near when anger
is deep and the furnace burns white.

the standard

she looked at the piano,
said "sometimes I hate that damn thing.
you can just disappear into music, and though you may
feel just fine, you can't forget me. you and that
goddamn piano."

he looked at the goddamn piano, tried to think of
it as an inanimate object—couldn't do it,
looked over at her and said
"sorry, could you repeat that?"

she shrieked. long and guttural.
a lovely shriek, filled with overtones,
glissandi and emotion, especially brief, door slamming
on the way out. a proper codetta.

he went to the piano, sat, rested his hands on the keys,
and spoke. "well, it seems we've done it again, eh?"
the piano didn't answer. he moved his hands.

body and soul   moonlight in vermont
love is just around the corner
the way you look tonight
lush life

there came his answer. he lit a cigarette,
closed his eyes,
smiled, placed his hands back on the keyboard.

where are you
sophisticated lady
stella by starlight
i only have eyes for you
always

then came some blues.

other angles

orbiting am I: a crawling sunset
across a bottomless sky:

coddling a new day's knife
through an old soul's geometry:

singing soul songs
of paralyzed civilization:

making love
to the moon and stars:

past the brittled roots,
the unfulfilled eye:

the startled moment when
i wake and feel the falling.

variations

the lettering on the window
      reads "village coffee shop"
behind the window sits
      a woman in a red blazer
reading a magazine while
      picking gently at a
thick slice of cheese cake.
      across the street behind
a window which reads
      "village tavern" he sits,
scotch in hand watching the
      red blazer, thinking she could
be the love of someones life—
            even his:
      eddie, the bartender delivers the
punch-line to his latest joke.
      everyone laughs half-heartedly,
he sits back and lets the
      whisky resume its burn.

the man in the black suit

        sporting an electric blue versace tie
celebrates the final night of
    life   he glides across the carpet
  in handmade alligator pumps   pretending not a
care
      contemplating his gibson (extra dry) —

bowing to his wife (as she flirts with a dark latin man)
    he makes his way to the terrace and
climbs over the rail   feeling queasy
    due to a life long fear of high places

he straightens himself   gulps the drink
    and enters space   with all grace
and aplomb akin to his station in life

blackout

    no televisions' blare
    no music from stereos—
opening my apartment door
    i check on the old
    couple across the hall—
"probably be on in a few minutes"
    charlie tells me—
    i nod, close my door
then rummage through the pantry
    for a candle—finding one
    but also finding a
framed picture of my once-love
    i had hidden years ago…
i do not see it in the dark, i only recall the feel of its metal frame.
    i replace it and search for matches,
    find them, trip my way to the living room
breathing relief after lighting the solitary torch:
    the window, chair and bookcase
    pulsed in light, the shadow
of my hands making notes on the wall—
    I close my eyes
    and sing of lost love,
celebrating the madness of my being there.

the fall

she can't sleep,
   nowhere is release;
hours fall yet no

   peace. how to get
from there to here?
   upstairs neighbor paces,
obviously
       flustered:

she didn't know he
   disliked
monteverdi on the stereo
   at 1 a.m.

he might be angry,
   but like many
       neighboring
   in houston

the worst that could
   pass might be a
     smirk adorning

the obvious.
  "another
    hot one,
       eh?"

monteverdi plays
   on. her cigarette smoke
           rises.

eyes follow
  a ceiling
 shuddering in disrespect.

red

the crepe myrtles
reach
a hand to heaven
outside my bedroom
window

inside
my love reaches for
strawberries in
a bowl

she follows the
tree lines
chewing intently

whirling her
mind suddenly reacts
a
hushed dribble
i startle her

closing the bedroom door

the wind

carrying the cloaked message barely present enough
to kiss a cheek,   powerful enough
to knock out power lines or awaken dark sleep.

the wind coming off the long island sound...
bridgeport in january... bridgeport in decay...
dressed in overtones... adorned in ridicule
and magic: telephone lines and bushes in
sudden ice framing a moment where all you could do
was listen—the factories closed for the day. listen...
the street lights still on at 3 in the afternoon.

three black men huddled in the doorway of maloney's bar—
still an hour before she's open and warm.
when the wind cried   i sang along, wanting no place to go.

eugene

it is the scent
        of wet earth
and the sound of his
        feet crushing it—

he says his prayer
        then comes a silent shiver:
the rain will deliver
        more than is needed.

humming and old melody
        from his grandfather
he feigns insanity for a moment
        then shakes it away—

an ambulance screams
        a cufflink drops
a thunderclap
        ave maria on the radio:

he recalls a viscous joke
        told by a distant cousin
years ago when he was
        less than sober:

now and then
        he thinks of
being married
        but he feels secure

cufflink in place
        he is on his way
to a job he once would
        have mocked—

opening the ridiculous umbrella
        inhaling the thick air
treading to the bus stop
        mumbling at his feet

then once arrived, sniffs
        the cheap perfume
of a stringy-haired girl of 20 yrs.
        breathes in her double-deep

it is now his day—
        his shoes quite damp
the song on his lips
        continuing

hannah

long gone far away
the red haired girl

knee deep in plaids and
snowdrift, sniffled into scented

linen, moved with the filament
grace of satie's gnossiennes,

bathed in the colors of daylight,
knee deep in plaids

with her catholic
school overbite.

post-funeral

weird uncle frank
        didn't remember me

kayla crying in the back yard
        wanting to play with the other
little ones

roast chicken, string-beans, cake,
        teenagers understanding,
but not quite enough

the dead man's younger brother
        yanking off his tie

the sky leaning to overcast:
        aunt ann takes out the garbage: in

the comic whirl of grief
        uncle frank stuffs his face,
silently insane

nothing by it

the music wailed,
it should have whispered—

her green dress
screamed in black.

she danced a jig,
ate a fugue, then

reneged on introductions
to the bereaved family,

having forgotten their names.

tonight

it is the 3rd symphony
of roy harris

that really hits the nerve.
how could one hear this music

and not sense the triumph and
      despair of poor folk or
          the premature deaths of great men?

      it is almost enough to forgive
the weight of time

      and its failure
      to cure.

oh, but our own

the bar smells of
sweat—stale and pure, honest

as a tree leaden in memorial
timber. faces comforted in

sameliness, furrowed and red-cheeked;
never far to go, always near home,

the heart alone.
here good companions

creak back and forth
on wooden stools.

for them the smells
are everyday.

the eyes speak truth.
hit'em again.

good morning

       no, this is not innocence, no youthful prank nor
clasping of lover's hands at the twilight. we have
       nurtured the seed but not raised the dead.
not in the onion held to the bright sky, peeled slowly
       away to reveal its gentle prize, its gentle nothing;
not in the veins and arteries jetting fruit and sinew
       coursing their juice back and forth without pause;
simply the end song, the birth charm, and in-between,
       the folly.

elusive memory

it struck me in the grocery store
while i meandered over what
to do for dinner—
      she was standing, contemplating
      two brands of light bulbs;
her porcelain features, light brown page boy
hair, slight of frame; so delicate.
      i passed as close as i dared
      just to smell her hair
      if i could—nantucket briar—
      i could have sworn
      or maybe i just wanted it to be.
the thing is,
it wasn't her,
yet i still look for her.
it's been years since she moved to the tiny
vermont town while I remained in the
baked city of houston.
years since we have spoken.
still, i look for her; our time together was good and
it is necessary for me to look.
it is balance. now i am hungry and i think
lamb stew is just the thing.

portrait in two yellows

the milkweed hangs in the thick houston air
        like a perverse snow, unmelting, just
coming to rest on car hoods and shrubberies.
        and life goes a bit slow on richmond ave:
traffic funnels from three lanes, then two, finally
        one. jackhammers rattle, shovels scrape,
the men working them, their skin brown leather,
        not sweating. years of this toil makes

them immune. they will eat hot peppers with their
        lunch and drink hot black coffee, huddling
in a deceptive shade; those in the cars
        with their radios blaring, their phones
ringing, their air conditioning humming, will pass and
        not realize the contrast of two distinct
environments until they park and take the tortuous
        twenty-three steps to their office lobby.

john kerrigan steps from his car, locks the door, checks
        his watch, turning to the street as the veil of horns
gives testimony to a third light change
        not made. he chuckles at the sad mardi-gras
then shuffles into the cuban market to buy his cigarettes.
        two mexican youths, heads shaved, meander
in the doorway, dropping their eyes as john passes through.
        back on the street, traffic has dead-stopped
and those in the cars fidget, then find their special song.

the florist

i often think of dion o'banion,
the smiling irish gangster from chicago.
i remember seeing his picture in a book
when i was 12 yrs. old. he didn't
look like a man who had seen to the death of
at least 25 other men. i read
the book and learned that he
and his companions hymie weiss,
schemer drucci and bugs moran
were
the real lords of chicago during the early years
of prohibition. they were courted by politicians,
fawned over by the press, and, omitting those
trampled and crushed by them, adored by the locals.

deany supplied the highest quality booze in town.
i have seen other pictures,
and in them his boyish charm still shines through. his eyes,
squinting, exhorting "c'mon now, it was all in fun."
he owned a flower shop, fashioned
gaudy wreaths for gangster funerals,
chortling among the lilies.

his own end came in that very shop, november, 1924.
his enemies could not abide his rhapsodic ways.
with millions to be made in rotgut and needle
beer, life was not a jig, but an opera.

al capone may have been the biggest of all,
but it was deany o'banion who kept the boys in
stitches
when it really counted.

neutral adhesive

in opus 111 beethoven reached
the 20th century—he is swinging,
      almost like basie
but it is innocent, maybe even a mistake.
    when gershwin, copland and
stravinsky tried their hand at jazz
      the results were disastrous,
            pointless.
the critics like to remember those kind of failures.
    I'd rather think of beethoven, miles davis
and paul klee sitting at a table in a new york nightclub
      making goo-goo eyes at maria callas.

bridgeport

1

the blind man
playing guitar
(whose name
not I
nor do i think

anyone else
floating bye
and bye recalled)

as
the August moon
blushed
as the steel sky
yawned to God
but
then
we do remember

2

before
the dead walk
she said
wade out into the
water then suddenly turn
when

you taste the
salt and feel pantomime
hosts tickle and slice at
your legs and the soles of your feet
then you will know (if you want
to know) alive

And then I said
now make
the dead dance

3

three rooms that face the ocean.
two children
glum
emotion(less)
cause (repent) this hanging
fan
this breezing
forget(full of me)
leaflessly
The trees,
their bones (without enough effect)
splatter on windows of

4

these so called memories
baked and chiseled
so
deep
in the soft folds of
alone as
(i don't know)
a phone rings
a book falls from
a hand to the floor
and

the
grip of death
focuses again

5

the naked wind
kissing
the
rusted clock
then
singing:
    truth; the rapier
    wit (denied)

6

love (they say)
can move
mountains

but (i say)
can it ease
the pain
of cancer

ah (she says)
love conquers
all

oh (i say)
to be
conquered by
any old thing
but

7

inch
be (come closer)
of (fool's
betrayal) inch
am (away)
only if
am be
(intrepid)
disappeared.

8

once in cold
december (colder
november was) i
watched a man
slowly dying (i was
so close to it) his
horrible disease
his matter-of-factly
smiles
his eyes (so cold)
his eyes
probing the air like a knife

never wanting anything
not about to
give in then
stop.

9

transfer affection
ancient to
anxious

whose name

(knifed in tendril
shrieked in stone)

home called
none alone (pale
away)
away,
too away
to

10

as in streets
crumbling
divinity   (pause)
a weakness (holdfast
the child & dog
sharing ice pop)
falling away
but suddenly not now
exists only as
its own

11

so very sad
so weak his lungs'
breath reflex (like us
gently criminal)

and when i asked "are you
scared?" he turned
away ignoring
me

such stupid things
one can say
at such stupid
times
it seems

12

a man's nightmares

streets closed
laughter somewhat

dirty overcoat
eyes looking away

She's not (there)
home (anywhere)
but the laughter

(is it hers?) the
silent prison (search)
only you hold the

sanctity

of your
own (burn of
aloneness) forgetting

requiem for a jazz club

it stood on elgin blvd, was open
barely a year but so many great ones passed through
you could see a universe on any given night

this was the club that pulsed—everything in tempo
      I fell in love at lott's place every night
      and I was there every night
      and it was easy every night

                a tempo:
there were carl and lilly lott greeting guests
then carl off to the bandstand to the drumset
ready to call the first set

cousin herman worked the door and
he could tell you a history of jazz
not found in any textbook

carl jr behind the bar—june we called him
and drinks were mixed and served
according to the tempo set by the music

when arnett cobb played
it was a rich medium pace
don wilkerson—double time

and the elegant lilly waving a graceful
finger at arriving patrons
"yes, there is a cover charge
no, there will be no sitting in tonight
this is a business
not a living room"

there were cousins, cousin's wives, nephews,
aunts and uncles—all had their specific duties

there were poets in the kitchen
scotch and laughter
pots bubbled with creole

> we ate well at lott's emporium club café and
> best was the boudin so damn hot you had
> to bathe it in tabasco which amazingly cooled it down
> a notch (a little trick I learned from june)

oh that sweet pulse of lott's place:

arnett cobb
perched on aluminum crutches
suit and tie
soul singing
mad howling
the medium groove
whispers to silent suns
sermons to angry moons

don wilkerson
the mumbling prophet
tearin' greased lightning
hard-bop
out of the tenor sax
a frail sickly cat
endowed with
herculean endurance
when the horn
was in his mouth
when the rhythm section popped
and for don we popped

the gray beard
pharoah sanders
who rarely
spoke a word
except through the horn
but one night
shook the walls
when he grabbed
the mic and shrieked
"I got the blues
I got the blues
lord knows
I got the blues"

and every night smiling faces,
sexual nerve-burning energy
busting for revelation
seeding the air
careening of the walls
those fine blackbrownwhite
beauties framed in night and the
color of dare and escape

when hank crawford played
his coterie followed
whoopin' hollerin' testifyin'

one could never forget the
4 sisters (not a one of 'em
under 300 lbs)
dominating the scene
and every time hank would twist a blue phrase
out of his alto how they would wail along

The drinks tasted different at lott's
      the scotch was brighter
the mood was different at lott's
      people were tolerable or tolerant

and back then I was the skinny balding piano player
who just had to be there and to hell with the bread
      and the bass player my ex-brother-in-law
and I would drive together every night 'cause it was
      a bad part of town outside but inside
was a groove

and now
kisses to you
carl & lilly
and june and rae and herman
and all those beautiful musical cats

my belly is still full from crayfish, boudin, chicken & rice,
until we meet again
the fire still burns
the water still boils
at lott's emporium jazz club cafe

modern english

sad eyes in midwinter, holding a styrofoam cup
        filled with coffee. I smiled at you so
you came over and talked as if you knew me.

you told me of your children, your ex-husband,
        the courses you take at the community
college—you were so animated, the coffee would

jump from the cup and I would step backward
        then you would step forward and the
others standing near were curious but glad

to be uninvolved. all I could think was why me?
        all I wanted to do was continue running
lee morgan's solo on blue train over and over in my mind.

exercises for independence of the fingers

i hear the great ones:
bach, mozart, beethoven,
mahler, stravinsky,
schoenberg—on and on,
the vortex europa

and in the crosswinds
comes jazz, my jazz,
and it is home.

george washington, baby,
george

fats waller

ear to ear grin.
great wide belly.
fingers invisible
whirling.

joy
drunk in love.

snickering
cartoon.

sinister eyebrows,
taunting
the devil.

genie. genius.

grandmother

near the end
her eyes could
barely make out
the images on the t.v.,

but she could hear
the grunts of the
wrestlers

and loved it when
the great sammartino
would talk in italian
to his italian friends
out in t.v. land

gesturing madly
on about the miller
brothers,

argentina apollo,
bulldog brower,
fred blassie.

it was a simple life,
then

she died,
and i had to grow up,

and

i didn't want to.

father

he is religious
doesn't go to church
drinks too much coffee
won't buy water
                "are you gonna fix
             that light switch or
         maybe you just
     like being in the dark."
he is a candle
glows just right
               (when you think he sleeps)
lighting another pall-mall
a breaking flame
just when you knew
you had figured him out
        smiles away brilliantly
      planning his distances
     planning his angles
stress is rust
can't dream on rust
god knows he has tried

stone idol

like some
strung out
college professor
you sat staring
into a souls
cold terrain.

it seemed as
though you
weren't breathing,
then suddenly,

automatically,

you picked up
a scarred trumpet

and started to
blow
streams of bitterness
and consciousness

that forced anyone
with the nerve to listen

to remember their
own souls

and remain thankful
for having
the cold to touch.

i've missed you
chet baker,

more than i ever
thought i would.

an occasional gentleman

he was
not an old man
just a young man
      feeling old
sitting
at the piano
playing the opening lines
      of the way you look tonight
thinking
    "nothing left—
      nothing left
        at all"
the weight of the keys   seem
    too much   too much
        too
scared   he feels   while
recalling so many times
feeling this way   before—
        yet at the
        point of giving in
        a sudden reprieve—
sanctity—
power
returning to him: bringing him back
        to himself.
on and on the song goes,
upside down under the mistletoe.

like gieseking playing scarlatti

"it is in the teapot
above the
basement sink.
Don't be afraid."

i found the teapot,
it was empty.

years after
her passing i
recalled its emptiness

and in it found
her final breath.
her pure gift.

faceless in texas

to dream of simple things
        if only i could dream such things
i wish i could, but memories

        from another time another place
i dream too deep
        i wish i could just dream good day

i wish good sleep

a wave of despair

pinions me
>   yet i drag my feet

along the tile floor
>   of the shopping mall,

trying to decide: will a new tie,
>   some after-shave, a new

suit or a chance encounter
>   with a mexican cleaning

woman bring me back to
>   my smiling self ?

when i write music

the best moment comes
when a melody is realized.

i quickly scribble it down,
play it a few times and in

that sudden instant experience
an incredible rush of aliveness.

occasionally a rare melody will
come, one where i know instantly

that i have tapped into the soul.
i might even think of jumping up

on the piano bench and doing a
can-can, though i haven't as yet.

the manuscript will rest on the piano
for perhaps weeks, coming under

repeated playings and rewritings (the
rare ones never need rewriting.) if it

endures, i will put it into process:
copy it neatly, rehearse it, perform it,

record it, perform it some more. each of
these steps taking me further away

from the precious first moment,
inevitably leaving me empty,

wanting for new melodies.
thinking they must come soon.

ecology

since
chopin

piano
poetry

since
hendrix

guitar
science
fiction

in our greed

we find art
in nothingness

then connect to it
the pain

of needing
so much more

sudden heart

tones from
a piano

suspended in
night air
stillness.

*

quizzical
dragonflies,

sculptured
in
division.

eulogy

oblique asshole
more interesting
than other parts:

constipated voices,
foreboding farts.

Lyrics

flamingos

the silent screaming
of lonely souls
seeking justice
under willow trees
or in collision
with speeding vehicles
will not remain silent.

in loving light (the silent screaming)
or dreaming blackness, (of lonely souls)
patiently waiting for us,
watering our lawns,
pissing away our substance.

silent silence.

st. john

down the narrow cobbled street,
a single light in a shop window.
an old man reads his bible
well past closing time.

outside the madmen
hide in growing shadows
swallowing beer from brown sacks.
making scenery which plays over and over,
through time framed in plague and prosperity.

the doors of the church left open.
the final evening song of birds
on telephone wires
cackling in rumor and relief.

the old man lays down his book,
rubs his eyes, flips on the radio
cueing the shutdown ritual
to the strains of the st. john passion.

la divina
for m.c.

she's known things that looked and felt
and even pulsed and beat like the human heart,
and now she doesn't know
what has become of her, where did she go?
she doesn't know if she's herself
or is it dreaming.
she must be dreaming.

oh, how the moment drags on,
this cocktail hour's a hell,
they raise their glasses to her,
she bows, falls to her knees,
they laugh, they think she jokes.
what they don't know is killing her,
she's not herself today or ever.
she must be dreaming.

the sky is screaming.
the moon is preening.
the winds are scheming.

eugene

a week and three days behind in rent.
crumpled pack of cigarettes on the floor.
can't remember how or why,
wife left 3 days ago,
could have been 5 years ago.
each hour's an anthem.
each night an orchard,
each moment a lament.

photographs gathering dust on the floor,
next to the broken glass from the panel on the door.
can't remember how or why,
wife left 3 days ago,
could have been 5 years ago.
each hour's an anthem.
each night an orchard,
each moment a lament.

eugene cuts his hair with a kitchen knife.
tries to look presentable for his wife
she could have a change of heart!

the phone's turned off, but there's no one to call,
so he straightens up the pictures on the wall.
can't remember how or why,
wife left 3 days ago,
could have been 5 years ago.
each hour's an anthem.
each night an orchard,
each moment a regret.

eugene turns on channel 3 hoping for the news.
all he manages to find are some clues
to a confusing world.

the neighbor next door mows the lawn.
everything seems so right it must be wrong
can't remember how or why,
wife left 3 days ago,
could have been 5 years ago.
each hour's an anthem.
each night an orchard,
each flower a lament.

again

you will say you're leaving
i will ask "how soon?"
you will grab your keys and
i will leave the room,
but will ask, "is this it,
are you gone for good?"
oh, away you go.
goodbye.

will you please take the cat?
never liked the cat.
it is cold outside so
wear your woolen hat.
supper will be held
in case you should come back.
i won't hold my breath
too long.

why do you still stand there?
are you feeling ill?
come in, close the door
before you catch a chill
now I'll light the candle
on the windowsill.
oh, my love,
welcome home.

oh, my love,
welcome home.

oh, my love,
welcome home.

Lovecraft On The Beach

Mister looks out from his window,
Watches the leaves dance in the breeze.
Shakes a smile, picks up his pencil,
Thinks about the monsters in the trees.

Sees himself standing in the ocean,
Hears the flutes off in the distance.
Comes the dark, voices whisper.
In the dark, voices whisper.

Mister has written a letter
To someone he would never meet.
Auntie serves tea in the parlor,
Life is good, but often bittersweet…

Winding his way through the gray streets,
Hears the chant coming from the ocean.
Quiet night drowned in seclusion,
Fading light bathed in illusion.

For You

There is a voice, there is a key
and the moon in the mirror
Then a face behind the glass
A tiny shadow on the river.

Unlike the wolf, it howls at noon.
Another stone in the ocean.
Under the sky it stands alone
Inside a cloud without motion.

This and so much more
It will hold for you.

Like the rain upon the sand,
Like the poem wrought in sadness,
To drive alone so far from home
and rejoice in the madness.

Oh so near you are, my dear
It breathes in your emotion.
Little while before the smile
Many miles to the ocean.

This and so much more
It will hold for you.

Then ride a camel 'round the world
But I can't say you will like it.
A crazy trip, don't lose your grip,
'cause there's no other ride like it.

Ride a falcon through the sky,
Find a fortune in starlight.
Read the runes etched on the moon,
Touch the secret to midnight.

This and so much more
It will hold for you.

And once returned you may have learned
The only story worth hearing
Is of a child who stays a child
When the world has gone weary.

Now and then, go back again
To the show that's worth showing.
Forget the hat, forget the coat,
It is warm in the gloaming.

This and so much more
It will hold for you.

One I Hope to Love

In the light of a quiet moon
I would wait by my door
And if I see you there
I'd try not to stare,
You're so easy on the eyes
If not the heart.

If you pass will you notice me?
I could hope for a glance.
A simple nod would do.
Would I fall for you?
It would be so easy to give in,
I would not ever be indifferent
To one I hope to love.

Ghosts

In a most secluded place
Where lover's dreams come commonplace
Where children dance with awkward grace
For queens adorned in faded lace
And far beneath the flowered domes
Some rustle in their crowded homes
They stare at those left all alone
They hide what simple things they own

Secret sister, little clown
Freckles and a scarlet gown
Reads her good book upside-down
Sings but doesn't make a sound
Somewhere near the voices call
Up the stairs and down the hall
Ancient pictures on a wall
Waltzes at a midnight ball

Paralyzed

you drive your car
to the edge
of the canyon,
cry a name
hear an echo.

you sit in church
feeling numb
when it crosses
past the altar
during vespers.

In the night
Something wrong
Feel no future
Feel no song
Stoically when dreams have broken
We ask for rain
When only hurt remains.

unleash the wolves,
let them feed.
such injustice
in the theater
of denial.

In the night
Something wrong
Feel no future
Feel no song
Stoically when dreams have broken
We ask for rain
When only hurt remains.

spectacular,
c'est magnifique,
as the animals retreat
to the barnyard.

Not Far Away

No one knows
Will she go or stay
She can be so blasé
Yet, in her eyes
Truth and lies reside
Such a mystery
I can almost see
She's not far away
Not far away

A Widow's Tale

So like a child
She is wanting,
Much like a child.

So like a child
She is needing,
Much like a child

Lonely afterthoughts,
Mid-life crises.
Wine and a thousand dreams,
Be still, be still.

Talk to me now,
Tell a story,
Talk to me now.

Speak as a child
Who is keeping
Thoughts of a child.

Moon above the skies,
Cold and yearning.
Anger in your eyes,
Be still, be still.

Sideshow

The curtain pulled aside,
The whisp'ring in the crowd.
And the show begins
When the lights have dimmed.
Before our eyes
Wonders take shape then dance
And disappear.

Comes the Rain

Long ago,
Our hearts were young,
I danced in the rain.

Now skies get dark
I stay inside
And watch the rain.

I'm really not afraid,
I just don't want to ruin
The fantasy of youth.

So comes the rain
Perhaps I'll be
My old self again.

Scary People

Whistling in the dark
Try'n to keep my mind
From wand'ring.

Things just seem so bleak
In the dark.

I think I shall stay
Right where I am

'way from scary, scary people

Waiting in the dark
Try'n to keep my heart
From jumping

The light is very weak,
Very cold

I think I shall stay
Right where I am

'way from scary, scary people

Ms. Thing

Too tired to sleep
She lingers by the window,
and wonders... .
Old books collect in a corner.

Why must it always be?
No one to call,
Not one to worry, still,

Dear Ms. Thing,
Don't feel so precious.
Fix your smile,
Adjust your glasses.

Too tired to cry
She puts away her photos,
      and wonders... .
Shadows grow mean in the corner;

Lit by a curious moon.
She tries to call
No one remembers her name

Ms. Thing,
Don't feel so precious.
Fix your smile,
Adjust your glasses.

Clear your throat
And smooth your hair
Then walk into
The cold night air.

Dear Ms. Thing,
Don't be afraid.
Don't be afraid.
Don't be afraid.

Acknowledgments

I wish to thank Michael Sofranko and Kurt Lovelace for their support and encouragement to publish this work. Without them, this book would only exist in a Word file on my computer.

I also thank some of the outstanding teachers who have assisted in my creative endeavors, among them Catherine Candela, Winifred LoCascio, Sr. Therese Damien Weber, David Barnett, Bob Preston, Neil Slater, Tony Campise, Arnett Cobb, Mike Nase, Frank Rehak, Dennis Dotson, Aubrey Tucker, Ed Soph, Art Lande, Phil Gurlik, and Christine Schaffer among many others.

Most of all, I thank my parents, Roy and Margaret LoCascio, who always offered encouragement in the paths I have chosen.

Joe LoCascio
April 2023

Joe LoCascio

Joe LoCascio has spent a lifetime creating and performing music. He is an award winning composer who has written for ensembles of all sizes and is prolific in both traditional and jazz genres. As a performer he has released 20 critically acclaimed jazz recordings, most containing his original compositions.

LoCascio and his wife Lucia currently reside in Houston, Texas. Joe is a full-time instructor of music at the Houston Community College.

AN OCCASIONAL GENTLEMEN'S NOTES is his first book of poetry.

Listen to Joe's Music

On Spotify:

https://open.spotify.com/artist/754Sb5i3y4ZUk8hweccYqV

On YouTube:

https://www.youtube.com/@joelocascio/videos

Also by Joe LoCascio

Books

THE JAZZ PIANO HANDBOOK
Tafford Publishing Inc (1992)

Selected Discography

Sleepless (w/Chet Baker) PAUSA PR-7200
Gliders - CMG CML 8002
Marionette - CMG CML 8015
In A Mist (The Music of Bix Beiderbecke) GSS 1040
Sleeping City - Optimism OP 3222
World With a View - Optimism OP 3232
Silent Motion - Tafford 1041
A Charmed Life - Tafford 2346
Home (Solo Piano) – Heart Music 0020-60018-2
Q – Tafford 4445
Close to So Far – Heart Music
The Late Show (w/Warren Sneed) – Pathways Music
In the City of Lost Things – Heart Music
Ghosts (Solo Piano) – Blue Bamboo Music
HCC Monday Night Big Band – **Music of Joe LoCascio**
Seasons Ago – The Songs of Alec Wilder
(w/Woody Witt) – Heart Music
Nameless Places (w/Patty Sanders) - Tafford Music
Absinthe – The Music of Billy Strayhorn
(w/Woody Witt) - Blue Bamboo Music
Book of Days – Independently Released
Chamber Music – Independent Digital Released
November (The Music of Phil Gurlik) – Tafford Records
Evidence (Music of Thelonious Monk) Solo Piano - Tafford Rec.
Postcards, North Babylon - Tafford Records
Blood and Bone (w/John Adams and Ed Soph) - Tafford Records

www.ingramcontent.com/pod-product-compliance
Lightning Source LLC
Chambersburg PA
CBHW020444090526
44586CB00045B/854